Memorial Day

By Sheri Dean

Gareth Stevens
Publishing

Please visit our Web site, www.garethstevens.com. For a free color catalog of all our high-quality books, call toll free 1-800-542-2595 or fax 1-877-542-2596.

Library of Congress Cataloging-in-Publication Data

Dean, Sheri.
  Memorial Day / Sheri Dean.
    p. cm. —(Our country's holidays)
  Includes bibliographical references and index.
  ISBN 978-1-4339-3921-1 (pbk.)
  ISBN 978-1-4339-3922-8 (6-pack)
  ISBN 978-1-4339-3920-4 (library binding)
  1. Memorial Day—Juvenile literature. I. Title.
  E642.D425 2011
  394.262—dc22
                            2010004599

New edition published 2011 by
Gareth Stevens Publishing
111 East 14th Street, Suite 349
New York, NY 10003

New text and images this edition copyright © 2011 Gareth Stevens Publishing

Original edition published 2006 by Weekly Reader® Books
An imprint of Gareth Stevens Publishing
Original edition text and images copyright © 2006 Gareth Stevens Publishing

Art direction: Haley Harasymiw, Tammy Gruenwald
Page layout: Daniel Hosek, Katherine A. Goedheer
Editorial direction: Kerri O'Donnell, Diane Laska Swanke

Photo credits: Cover, back cover, p. 1 Spencer Platt/Getty Images; p. 5 © Skjold Photographs; p. 7 © Otis Imboden/National Geographic Image Collection; pp. 9, 15 © AP/WIde World Photos; p. 11 Juan Barreto/AFP/Getty Images; pp. 13, 21 Shutterstock.com; p. 17 © Tom Prettyman/PhotoEdit; p. 19 © iStockphoto.

Printed in the United States of America

CPSIA compliance information: Batch #CS10GS: For further information contact Gareth Stevens, New York, New York at 1-800-542-2595.

Table of Contents

Boldface words appear in the glossary.

A Day to Remember

On Memorial Day, we remember the people who have died while fighting for our country in wars.

We think about how these people kept our country safe. We think about how they fought on land, at sea, and in the air.

'959

7

Showing Respect

We **celebrate** Memorial Day on the last Monday in May. We honor people who have died for our country. We put flowers and flags on their **graves**.

Some people put flowers on rivers, lakes, and seas, too. This is to honor the **sailors** who died at sea.

Some people buy special red paper flowers to wear. This shows their respect for those who fought and died for our country.

13

Half-Mast

On Memorial Day, our country's flag is flown at half-mast. This means it is put halfway down the **flagpole**. This is a way to honor the people who have died for our country.

15

Soldiers, sailors, and others who served our country are called the military. They march in parades on Memorial Day. Many people watch the parades.

Taking Time

On Memorial Day, many people take time off from school and work. They honor their family and friends who fought and died for our country.

On Memorial Day, many people take a few moments of **silence**. They remember those who have died. They also hope for peace in the world.

Index

About the Author

Sheri Dean is a school librarian in Milwaukee, Wisconsin. She was an elementary school teacher for 14 years. She enjoys introducing books and information to curious children and adults.